TEACH YOUR EASY BOOK

CATHERINE STORING

Published in the United States by Writing Made Simple Press
www.WrtingMadeSimple.Today

Cover: BRAND IT Beautifully
Editing: Exact Writing Services, LLC
Interior Design: WMS Press

The author of this book does not prescribe financial advice or promotes the use of any of the techniques as a method for financial, emotional, or medical problems without the advice of a physician, either directly or indirectly. The intent of the author is only to offer information of a general nature to help you in your quest for financial and spiritual growth. In the event you use any of the information in this book for yourself, the author and the publisher assume no responsibility for your actions.

The 10-Step Formula to Teach Your Easy: How to Build Wealth by Teaching Others What Comes Naturally to YOU!

Published in the United States by WMS Press, Boston MA

For any ordering information or special discounts for bulk purchases, please contact WMS Press at catherine@catherinestoring.com

The 10-Step Formula to Teach Your Easy: How to Build Wealth by Teaching Others What Comes Naturally to YOU!

3rd edition, Feb 2019
Printed in the United States of America
ISBN # 978-1-7323425-4-5

TABLE OF CONTENTS

PART III

DEDICATION

I dedicate this book to every person that knows how to do something incredible but has taken it for granted for far too long. I know you are FINALLY ready to help other people by teaching them what you know, but also to monetize it and help yourself along the way. I pray that this book helps you see the value in your expertise and that it changes your whole entire life.

PART I

WHY I WROTE THIS BOOK

I am SO excited you are reading this book. It is TIME for you to FINALLY stop the endless cycle of:

- Not knowing how to make money
- Feeling guilty about wanting to make money
- Hating your 9 to 5 but not knowing what to do instead
- Starting and NEVER ending
- Undercharging for your products and services
- Playing hide and seek with you calling
- Looking at others wishing you could have what they have
- Wasting your gifts
- Dwelling in what's wrong
- Reminiscing on the "good old days"
- Living WAY below your means
- Making do and settling

If any or ALL of the above sounds familiar to you it is high time for you to step into your right place.

You were bought with a price [you were actually purchased with the precious blood of Jesus and made His own]. 1 Corinthians 6:20a AMP.

It is amazing just how long we put up with less than ideal situations. I should know; for years I just ACCEPTED that my little business would struggle. I did not question it. I just kept putting up with it. It was not a big deal because my corporate job subsidized the business and my thirst for learning. I did not REALLY need the money which is not a good place to be. Having too much or, worse yet, just enough KILLS the drive to thrive (in most instances anyway). But all that changed when I quit the hen with the golden eggs back on Tax Day, 2016. I will never forget that day; it was the scariest and most exhilarating day of my life. I would FINALLY be free to use my time as I saw fit and to make as much as money as I wanted. The issue was that after all that time (six long years, actually 11 years if we count the time, I tried my hand at being a fashion designer) I did not know how to make money. I knew how to work hard, and that I did VERY well. Can you relate? Do you have an excellent and admirable work ethic, but your bank accounts DO NOT reflect that? If that is the case, you are in the right place.

I know what you are thinking, "Catherine, there is no RUSH to read this book and implement the lessons inside of it, after all I have been under-earning for a VERY long time". I first saw that term when I read the book: "Overcoming Under-Earning", by Barbara Stanny (a must-read book by the way) and it really touched me, but it did not show me how to actually stop underearning in my business.

The truth is that you have been under-earning for far TOO long. You can't afford another day or hour of functioning like this. Why? Because there are people assigned to you, and you can only reach them when (not if) you have the monetary resources, time and creative freedom to minister to them. How is that you ask? Well simply put, in your current condition, do you have the time or the resources to help others? I am willing to guess you are barely able to take care of yourself. Am I right?

You really cannot afford to NOT learn this skill (making money that is) any longer. Time is of the essence and the help begins with yourself. Do me a favor, please make a list of ALL the things you are in need of and put a price next to it. See an example below:

Groceries	$150
New car Down payment	$2,000
Utilities	$950
Tax Bill	$1040
Credit Cards	$375
Relative Loan	$600
Business Invoice 1	$250
Business Invoice 2	$344
Moving Expenses	$5,500
Business Updates	$450
Other	$500

You get the idea? Just imagine now that God provides you with ALL the money you need. Like, ALL of it. How would that feel? Amazing right? The truth is that He has already. You are mega rich already. He has given you SO many gifts and talents and He is expecting you to use them. ALL of them. They are a gift to you, but they cost Him a LOT. As you saw in 1 Corinthians 6:20a. They are free to you but that does not in any way diminish their value and worth.

Just imagine now if God were to tap you on the shoulder (first you might get very scared, but after the shock wears off you might get very excited), and asked you, "How are you my child? How are you using ALL the gifts I gave you to grow the Kingdom?" WOW! What a question, what would you say to that?

THIS IS WHY WE ARE HERE TO HELP OTHERS AND BE HAPPY ABOUT IT

One early morning while reading my Bible this passage in the book of Philippians hit me right between the eyes. Granted, I had read it before, but maybe because I read it in the Message version or because I was ready I saw it differently. Either way, I thought the words were very fitting and I knew I just HAD to share them with you.

> *1-4 If you've gotten anything at all out of following Christ, if his love has made any difference in your life, if being in a community of the Spirit means anything to you, if you have a heart, if you care—then do me a favor: Agree with each other, love each other, be deep-spirited friends. Don't push your way to the front; don't sweet-talk your way to the top. Put yourself aside, and help others get ahead. Don't be obsessed with getting your own advantage. Forget yourselves long enough to lend a helping hand.*

> *5-8 Think of yourselves the way Christ Jesus thought of himself. He had equal status with God but didn't think so much of himself that he had to cling to the advantages of that status no matter what. Not at all. When the time came, he set aside the privileges of deity and took on the status of a slave, became human! Having become human, he stayed human. It was an incredibly humbling process. He didn't claim special privileges. Instead, he lived a selfless, obedient life and then died a selfless, obedient death—and the worst kind of death at that—a crucifixion.*

> *9-11 Because of that obedience, God lifted him high and honored him far beyond anyone or anything, ever, so that all created beings in heaven and on earth—even those long ago dead and buried—will bow in worship before this Jesus Christ and call out in praise that he is the Master of all, to the glorious honor of God the Father.*

> *—Philippians 2:1-11*

Just like the passage eloquently explains we are to look out for one another, and that includes sharing with them what we know. Let us not take for granted that they already know what we know or that they don't need it. We are all part of the same body and, as such, ought to look out for each other. I pray this book helps you see the importance of what you know.

MINDSET WORK: WHAT IS YOUR IDENTITY?

This might be my favorite part of the entire book (you should know I say that about just every section, but this is truly one of my favorites), and the reason it is one of my favorites is because it encompasses three principles that changed how I saw myself and I pray it'll change how you see yourself also.

The three principles are:

1. We are citizens of heaven
2. We have access to the Common Wealth of heaven
3. We were created to rule/dominate the earth

Now that we have outlined each principle, let's look at each one in detail.

We Are Citizens of Heaven

> *But there's far more to life for us. We're citizens of high heaven! We're waiting the arrival of the Savior, the Master, Jesus Christ, who will transform our earthy bodies into glorious bodies like his own.*
>
> *—Philippians 3:20-21 MSG*

What does that even mean, right? It can be confusing; we live here on earth but because we were born again in Jesus Christ, we are now citizens of the kingdom of heaven. What are the benefits of such citizenship? You know we have access to **everything** in heaven, right? Well, you do.

According to Dictionary.com, citizenship is:

> *"the state of being vested with the rights, privileges, and duties of a citizen."*

What does that mean to you? The moment you said yes to Jesus you became FULLY vested; you gained access to the resources of heaven. In other words, **you do not have to walk around like you are destitute. You've got everything you need; you just need to ask.**

"Don't bargain with God. Be direct. Ask for what you need. This isn't a cat-and-mouse, hide-and-seek game we're in. If your child asks for bread, do you trick him with sawdust? If he asks for fish, do you scare him with a live snake on his plate? As bad as you are, you wouldn't think of such a thing. You're at least decent to your own children. So don't you think the God who conceived you in love will be even better?

—Matthew 7:7-11 MSG

One of the many things I love about being a citizen of the United States of America is the endless benefits available to me. One for example, I cannot be deported. As a citizen I get to stay here until the day I die or the day of Jesus Christ.

The other right I am kind fond of is that I have the right to express myself and the right to worship without fear of being persecuted. How amazing is that? Those are just two of the benefits to which I gained access when I became an American citizen.

When you became a Christian, you also became a citizen of heaven and, as such, you too have many benefits. You became royalty. Really? Yes, really. If your Father is the King, then you are royalty and as such have access to everything that belongs to the King.

However, not everyone believes or behaves as the son or daughter of the Most High King. How do I know? Because their lives do not reflect the kingdom of God. Their speech and mentality do not reflect it either.

I was talking to someone the other day. I confessed to her that it took me a minute to change my mindset about money and what was available to me. See, I had struggled my whole life. When I got married my life changed for the better. I was exposed to a world I had not seen before. Life was good. I adapted quickly to that lifestyle. **But then sadly came the divorce and I went back to Struggleville. I went back to a life of lack and barely enough. It was easy. Why? I had been there before. It was what I knew.**

Then I got a six-figure corporate career. Life was good again, but it took me longer to adjust because the struggle lasted too long the last time. My mind had gotten too comfortable in going without. It became my "normal." **I had to do some serious hard work internally to reclaim my kingdom identity. How do you that? You have to go back to the source and learn or be reminded of who you are and what God says about you.** Where can you find that? The Bible is the best place to find out what God says about you and about Himself. Last year I wrote the book: I Am Set FREE: Write Your Way to Lasting Wealth. Writing the book took me on a wild journey. I shared many supporting scriptures inside the book (pick it up next time you are on Amazon).

Once you get the book, meditate on those scriptures, as a matter of fact, take a screenshot of all the scriptures with your phone and bring them up every time (not if) small thinking, lack or fear in the areas of money, resources or your identity try to creep in.

We Have Access to the Common Wealth of Heaven

You have probably heard the word commonwealth before but probably have not stopped to think about its meaning. I heard someone talk about it the other day and it really blessed me. Let me try to break it down as God revealed it to me. When I heard the word split into two words something quickened in my spirit.

Common Wealth – if you were to look up the word **common** on Google you might find the following: occurring, found, or done often; prevalent.

If you were to look up the word **wealth** you might find: an abundance of valuable possessions or money.

Now if we were to put that together it might sound something like this: **often found or prevalent abundance of valuables or money.**

That sounds pretty good to me. How about to you? If we have access to EVERYTHING that belongs to the King, then that includes His wealth. What does God own? Let's see what the Bible says about that.

> *The earth is the Lord's, and everything in it. The world and all its people belong to him. For he laid the earth's foundation on the seas and built it on the ocean depths.*
> *—Psalms 24:1-2 NLT*

I don't know about you, but that scripture seems to tell me that my Daddy is the owner of EVERTHING and since I am an heir with Christ…how do I know that?

> *This resurrection life you received from God is not a timid, grave-tending life. It's adventurously expectant, greeting God with a childlike "What's next, Papa?" God's Spirit touches our spirits and confirms who we really are. We know who he is, and we know who we are: Father and children. And we know we are going to get what's coming to us—an unbelievable inheritance! We go through exactly what Christ goes through. If we go through the hard times with him, then we're certainly going to go through the good times with him!*
> *—Romans 8:15-17 MSG*

I think Romans explains our position in the Kingdom quite nicely. Why is it important that we understand this? Because I noticed that others (me included at some point) walk around with a destitute, hopeless, "this is my life forever" kind of attitude when, in fact, the COMPLETE opposite is true. I know what you might be thinking, "Catherine I have nothing going for me. I am SO broke and have no prospects." But if you were to look closer at your life you would notice God has given you some pretty awesome skills you can leverage.

> *So, my very dear friends, don't get thrown off course. Every desirable and beneficial gift comes out of heaven. The gifts are rivers of light cascading down from the Father of Light.*
> *—James 1:16-17 MSG*

At this point you might also be wondering why a how-to book has SO many scriptures and the answer is simple. **ALL the answers to what you are looking for are found in the Bible**. Your mindset will shift when you begin to consume the Bible's content on a regular basis. I know because my own mindset shifted when I read who God says I am. What did that do for me? It helped me stop thinking lack and fear were my portion.

Back to the gifts. God's gifts are perfect and VERY desirable. Your gift is unique to YOU. Yes, lots of people do similar things but they cannot do it like you. They do not have your background, flare, personality and calling. Take me for example, there are LOTS of writing coaches out there, like a gazillion, but how many of them have my background or have experienced what I have experienced? How many have my calling, combination of complementary gifts, and desire to help others tell their story and find their real self in the process? None of them. What does that have to do with you? My dear, you are unique. One of a kind. Multi-gifted and totally called for such a time as this. Let me share a little more about why you were created and then we can get on with the real reason why you bought this powerful and lifechanging book.

WE WERE CREATED TO RULE/ DOMINATE THE EARTH

I must be honest and admit I was not brought up or taught to believe this as a child. This concept is fairly new to me, but I am SO very glad the Holy Spirit brought me to the following scriptures and books like, Kingdom Citizenship by Dr. Myles Munroe. I would highly encourage you to pick up the audible version of the book. As a matter of fact, also become an Audible Member and listen to at least a book a month (your mind will be expanded and filled with content that edifies instead of listening to the dark and gloomy news the world loves to spew).

Let's start with these verses:

Then God said, "Let Us (Father, Son, Holy Spirit) make man in Our image, according to Our likeness [not physical, but a spiritual personality and moral likeness]; and let them have complete authority over the fish of the sea, the birds of the air, the cattle, and over the entire earth, and over everything that creeps and crawls on the earth."

27 So God created man in His own image, in the image and likeness of God He created him; male and female He created them.

28 And God blessed them [granting them certain authority] and said to them, "Be fruitful, multiply, and fill the earth, and subjugate it [putting it under your power]; and rule over (dominate) the fish of the sea, the birds of the air, and every living thing that moves upon the earth."

—Genesis 1:26-28 AMP

You made him to have dominion over the works of Your hands; You have put all things under his feet, 7 All sheep and oxen, And also the beasts of the field, 8 The birds of the air, and the fish of the sea, Whatever passes through the paths of the seas.

—Psalms 8:6-8 AMP

TEACH YOUR EASY BOOK

You, my friend were created to be in charge, to subjugate the earth and not the other way around. I was talking to someone the other day (this happens quite often) and they were telling me how much they hated their job but could not quit it. The person I was talking to had GREAT gifts and talents but did not know of a way to use said gifts and talents to not only replace his current salary but to actually surpass it. I am not judging the person. I too stayed at a job for far too long for the VERY same reasons. **To think I could have quit my soul-killing job much earlier could depress me, but I do not let it. I use it as fuel, and encouragement to help others recognize the importance of their gifts and how they were designed to provide a way to get ALL the resources they need.** The gift comes from God, the strength to do the work comes from God, the breath comes from God. Are you getting the picture? Once you let go of the "security" of a paycheck you will enter a new realm or payroll, if you will. You will join the MOST amazing workforce ever! You will be working for the Big Guy Himself. **As you begin to leverage your gifts you must also trust God to do what He said He would do**. That last part is VERY important.

Now that we have explored those three principles it is time to get started from THIS place. I wanted to make sure you understood the importance of the gifts God gave you. It is not a nice thing to do, but your duty; to use your gifts and talents, and to also share them with the world. Let's dig in, shall we?

INTRODUCTION

Welcome, I'm so excited. Oh, my God, I have been dying to put this book together for you for the longest time. And by that, I mean like for five days! Let me tell you how this book came to be, why I wrote it, and how you can use it. How does that sound? I was traveling for a conference; which could probably be the introduction to most of my previous books. I'm always traveling somewhere. I went to a conference, and it was amazing- and-a-half.

You know when you have high expectations by you get way more than what you expected? That's exactly what happened. I went to this conference called: The New Now Next Experience. If you haven't been to the New Now, Next experience, look it up; it'll bless your entire life. It is that amazing.

But anyway, I attended the conference because the founder is a good friend and I offered to help out in any way I could. I was not speaking at her conference so that gave me time to just blend in with the rest of the audience. Some people knew me, others didn't. While I was there, I began to see myself in a different light. Why? Because many of the people in attendance viewed me in a different light. Has that ever happened to you?

It is amazing how we sometimes take ourselves for granted. Sometimes, we do understand our value, but we get too comfortable with ourselves. It's not until somebody who doesn't know us, sees us for the first time. They marvel at all the things we can do. Their admiration reminds us to REALLY see our true selves and remember who we are. That's what happened at the conference. I think that's why we love to fall in love. When you think about it, it's not so much about loving the other person, which of course, is great. But when someone loves you, and they look at you with eyes that seem to say, "Oh my God, I cannot believe you are mine," and they think everything you do is wonderful, it reminds us of how amazing we are, and we love that. We love when someone other than ourselves sees us and recognizes us. Anyhow, back to the story...

I was at the conference having an amazing time minding my own business, praising, and worshiping. I couldn't even take notes because the speakers were so brilliant. I was there from Thursday night helping with setup 'til Saturday afternoon. When I got back to my friends' house, I was blown away. You know when you learned so much and you feel blown wide open in the best way possible? That's how I was feeling, and I was trying to put things together in my mind and figure out what was next. We had a powerful strategy session in which I helped her develop a $38,000-a-month strategy (I was tired but sometimes the best ideas come at those moments. That's how my brain works.)

After all that strategizing, my friend was like, "Oh, my God, I gotta go to bed." She just got up and left. I, on the other hand, couldn't go to bed. I was wired. And then I remembered something; a realization I had earlier in the day. In fact, I mentioned it to my spiritual mother who was also at the conference. I told her, "You guys don't even know what happened here this weekend. There are people here that are leaving completely transformed because now they get to do something that you have been doing your whole entire life. Your normal is not everybody else's normal."

When the thought came back to my mind, I really got it. I said it. It was my own quote. But it really hit me that night.

As I was writing and thinking, I said to myself, "That's it. My normal is not everybody else's normal." It really blew my mind. I told myself, "Okay, that is a book." And, if you know me or have met me before you know that I write books when I'm sitting down or going for a walk; the ideas just come to me, they just do.

I started writing the outline for the, "Your Normal Is Not Everybody Else's Normal", book (this was before the name was changed to, The 10-Step Formula to Teach Your Easy). I kept working on it and I was blown away while putting it together. It's just amazing how it was happening so fast.

And then I realized as I was typing, "Wait a minute, "Teach Your Easy". That's it! It comes easy to me because I've been doing it maybe my whole entire life. I don't think it's a big deal but for the people in the conference, or anybody else/anywhere else in the world is not easy for them. I've been sitting on this thing forever-and-a-half."

I want you to think about this, what is it that you know how to do; that is easy peasy for you? Like, you can do it when you are sick. When you are tired. When you are hungry. You can be amazing at that thing no matter the conditions. Don't think too hard because we are going to have an exercise where I'm going to walk you through the process of finding out what your easy is, and which one to teach first. I, for example, have many, many, many easies; no, I'm not bragging on myself. Wait until you see how many easies you have; it's going to blow your mind.

I had to figure out which one I was going to teach first. I have a series of, "How to books", just like this one that I'll write eventually. But this right here is the foundational book. This is the big daddy of the entire series. That's what you have to figure out. Which skill or process will be the first one, and then you build from there.

Let me tell you, you are about to learn strategies that are very advanced but worry not; I'm going to break them down for you. That's why I decided to speak this book first (that is how I first released the book, in audiobook format); I wanted the reader to receive it first. I don't want you to do any of the exercises. Yes, you may want to start with the manual, but I strongly encourage you to read (or listen) to this book at least once or twice. THEN begin working on the manual. It's amazing!

Here's why I want you to read it first. I'm going to speak this over your life. I want you to receive it. I want you to absorb it and I want you to believe that it is possible... for you. I know you. How? Because you are probably just like me. If I had given you the manual first - with ALL the many resources it contains – you'd probably skip over the stuff you think you don't need, am I right? You have done that before. I know I have. Well, I don't want you to do that. I really, really, really don't. I want you to receive this in the way that will be MOST beneficial for you because I'm the creator. I put this manual together. I know what you need. Not because I'm smarter or better than you. No! It's because in the past I have done it the wrong way many times. So, trust me when I say I know what I'm doing, that I'm going to break this process down for you so you can see it in action and avoid my mistakes. If you follow my instructions you should find yourself saying something like, "Yes, I can do that. Yes, I can."

Oh my God. I'm so excited. I can't wait to get into, "The 10-Step Formula to Teach Your Easy: How to Build Wealth by Teaching Others What Comes Naturally to You".

THE FORMULA EXAMPLE

Before I give you the formula, let me tell you that you are going to get apprehensive when the time comes for you to teach your easy. It's just the way it is. Even for me, as I prepared to put this together. I did all the pre-work. I laid the foundation. I did all the prep work and right before I was about to take the first step to record this content, I got a weird feeling in the pit of my stomach. That's normal; that just means you are alive.

I don't want you to think that you are having a heart attack. Unless you feel like you are, if that is the case then go see a doctor. But more than likely you are nervous. More than likely you are excited about what's next. And that is completely normal. I don't want you to get discouraged by this. I don't want you to be upset by this. It is the way it is. Don't worry. You are in the right place. Doing the right things. Got it? Okay, awesome.

Let me give you the formula first, then I'm going to break it down for you. What does that mean? I'm going to give you examples of what that it looks like. You know how sometimes someone explains something to you, but it makes no sense? Let me give you an example. Currently, I am in the middle of reading the book of Romans. I have read it before, but the Holy Spirit has me doing so again. Even though I am familiar with the material this time around it seemed like German to me. But there's a problem; I don't speak German. What did I do? I whipped out The Message Bible which that I learned as a young girl. Why? Because I didn't just want to read the book of Romans. It's not a race. I really wanted to internalize, understand, and get what I was reading. I read the book in the "hard version" first, and then I moved on to the "easy version" which made it so much better for me. I love them even though I have read them 10,055 times before.

I'm going to share The Formula below and then I'm going to explain each step-in detail. Got it?

1. **The Who & The What**: Figure to who and what you want to teach

2. **Storytelling**: Tell them who you are and why you are the person to teach them

3. **The Problem**: What's the pain they are experiencing today that you have ALSO experienced

4. **Your receipts**: Qualifications - what have you been through or learned along the way? (in a traditional school or the school of hard knocks).

5. **Your Step-by-Step Process Outline**: **VERY** high level though, Remember, less is more. You DO NOT want to overwhelm them.

6. **The Vehicle**: Decide how you are going to teach it: online, live, pre-recorded, in person, etc.

7. **The Teaching**: Teach each step thoroughly but do not beat a dead horse - easy does it

8. **The Product**: Logistics of creating, delivering and promoting the product or service.
   a. Write a description of your product that pops and makes people want to throw money at you
   b. Create an image that pops (if you don't know how to design, hire someone)
   c. What's the upgrade? - the nitty gritty
   d. Setup the pre-sale
   e. Promote, Promote, Promote
   f. Throughout the pre-sale and sales process ask questions and pay attention to what your future buyer is complaining about
   g. Add/tweak your product and process outline as you see fit

9. Create the product - keep it simple
   a. Deliver the product

10. Keep promoting it (Advanced)

That is it! I know that the 10-steps may sound like a lot right now, but I promise you, I am going to make this easy for you. I'm going to break this thing down for you one step at a time. Why? Because you want people to connect with you first. Let me tell you why.

Many times, when teaching a process or system we flow right into it. We go right into the meat and potatoes of the thing that we want to teach, but that's not how must people learn. Listen, in the beginning when first meet someone and begin to date, there is a period of wining and dining cute text messages, nice voicemails, flowers, gifts and food. Why? Because you have to warm up to each other. You have to get to know them. And let them get to know you. After all, they are already there; they are a captive audience. Entertain, baby entertain.

Storytelling: Who Am I helping? What Am I Teaching?

I love telling stories, which is why I'm a storyteller. But I was not always a good storyteller. And I did not always know what I wanted to do when I grew up. In fact, it took me about four decades to actually know what I wanted to do. I grew up on an island in the Caribbean which is why I have a 'faint' accent (depends on who you ask of course). I'm an island girl who grew up in a place where women were supposed to be quiet, have no opinions, and if they had opinions, they had to match the opinions of everybody else. I also did not look like the typical island woman. Because of that I was bullied; I was picked on, and I was ostracized in a way. So, very early on I knew that those were not my people. I love my island. I love my people. But I knew, "These people don't get me; these people are not where I expect to be in life." I always knew that I was going to move to the United States. I just knew I would find my people there.

Why did I think that? Because I had seen on TV, and read in books that in America, you could be an individual.

You could be anyone, be anything and do anything you wanted. I knew I was going to move there. I just knew it. Within a few years of this realization my family and I moved to the United States right before I turned 19 years old. I had to learn English as an adult. No problem. I've always been a hustler. I'm a very smart person. I am very intellectual. I knew I was going to learn the language, but in the process, I lost the fluidity of my native language. And along with that, I lost my writing voice.

Now, if you are going to be a writer, and you cannot write that's going to be a problem, right? It took me 19 years to find my writing voice again. It was painful as all get out. In the meantime, I had corporate job after corporate job, and although I was successful, I was miserable. The last job I had was as an IT Strategic Sourcing Manager. Yep, it is as boring as it sounds. But I was really good at it. God allowed them to train me really well, and thankfully I get to use all those skills and resources in my ministry and in my business today. So, don't feel sorry for me. Eventually I began to write books left and right, and that's all I thought I was supposed to do. Once I figured out how to finish books, I REALLY enjoyed the entire process.

However, without even knowing I put myself in a box, "I'm a writer." Then people began to push me outside of that box. I allowed myself to be pushed just far enough so I could begin teaching other people how to write books. I loved it. Oh, my God. I was in love. I love coaching, public speaking, and I love teaching. I thought, "This is great. My passion is writing. I love writing. I love teaching. This is it."

But in the back of my mind I kept thinking, "Is this all there is." I have always gotten strategy questions from my friends. I have always had a core group of people that would come and ask me questions, "Catherine, do you know how to do this or that?" Inevitably, I would say: "Oh, yeah, you just do this or that." This still happens on a regular basis - and I love it. But again, I was in a box. I didn't realize I had put myself in the, "You are a writer and a writing coach" box. And yes, those are things that I enjoy doing to this day. I'm passionate about them, but it's not all that I am.

I told you that I'm very smart. Well, I'm a nerd. I know nerdy things (by the way, I say that with pride, cause being a nerd used to have a negative connotation but not anymore. We nerds come in all sizes and colors and are TOTALLY proud of our nerdiness). I have always been a nerd. One of my favorite shows back in the day was The A-Team. Do you know that show? Check it out when you have some time. I'm totally dating myself, but hey, I watched it in Spanish way after it came out in the States so I'm not as old as that.

Anyway, I digress. Since watching the A-Team, I have loved computers and all the techie things they did. That was back in the late 80s, so, of course computers have come a long way since then. I loved it all. I also used to watch MacGyver in Spanish. I loved all the gadgets. I loved all of that.

Many of the things I know how to do in terms of looking at numbers, strategy, and how to put all of that together I learned WAY BEFORE I knew what I was called to do. Even how I recorded the audio version of this manual…I got my mic, sound guard, and everything that goes with it. And I figured all that out. I didn't go to school for any of it. I just figured it out.

Early in the manual I told you that the reason this came to me was because I went to a conference. What the conference did for me was destroyed the boxes I'd put myself in. I was blown away by that because I thought I was just a writing coach that happened to write books for myself and ghostwrite for others. I began to realize that I am much more than that. I'm really a teacher of many things. Just like I'm teaching you. "The Teach Your Easy Formula," as you read this book. I can teach many things.

I have a series of books that I'm putting together right after this one.

1. Stories that sell: Storytelling for People That Hate Selling But Have To

2. Project Management Made Easy: Get Your Project Done quickly

3. Live Stream Your Events Like A Pro

4. Why You Must Sell Your Product/Service

5. Launch it already

All those titles came to me in one day; seriously, the outlines, main idea; everything.

That's how my brain works. I've been sitting on that part of my gifts for a very long time. But not anymore. I am awake and it feels amazing. It feels freeing. As you hear my story, I hope that you'll see/begin to see yourself in a different light. Because maybe you too put yourself in a box. Maybe you too were taught that you were this or that; or were even limited to the things you could be when you grew up.

I was only taught that I was smart. My grades said that I was smart. The way I spoke said that I was smart. But I also wanted to be creative. Unfortunately, I was never encouraged to be more than smart. Being creative or artistic was not compatible with being smart. Well, I wanted to be both smart and creative. Why couldn't I be both? I can tell you today that I have learned to unleash my creative side. I still struggle with limiting beliefs because of the discouraging messages I heard growing up but it gets easier every day.

What box are you in right now? Have you been told that you are not creative or that you are not smart? Or maybe it's the opposite for you. Maybe you are a great painter, and that you should be a painter. But you don't want that to be your main source of income or your main thing. You want that gift to be one of your things. Something to think about.

Since the conference I have unleashed myself in ways I did not even know were possible. I am now officially teaching strategy to other coaches and business owners. Why? Because it comes naturally to me. And I enjoy it so very much. My brain just works at that speed. I'm able to see numbers, which I was not able to see before. How did that happen? I was trained to be strategic at my last job (even though I fought it with everything within me). Today, I love it and go out of my way to be strategic, not only in business but in life as well. I can tell you how much you should charge for a product or service. How much time you should spend putting it together, who would buy it, when they would buy it, how to present it, and how to package it all together. I know how to do ALL that. I asked myself, why am I not teaching all of this when I go live on social media or host a webinar?

This is how charged up I get when I talk about business and strategy. It does not matter where I am, whether I meet people in the train, online or in meetings. I'm like, "So what are you doing to grow your business? How much are you charging? And what do you want to be? How much money do you want to make? Have you monetized this yet?" We'll talk about that later in the book.

I want you to start seeing yourself in a different light. I really want you to start seeing yourself bigger and wider than you see yourself now. There is much more to you than what you have allowed yourself to see or others have seen in you. Does that make sense?

Things I used to hate before are the very things I really enjoy doing today. It is amazing how the brain works. I mentioned earlier that I started with knowing I was very smart. I explored that aspect of myself. Understanding that enabled me to become fluent enough in English to start taking college level classes within a year of moving to the States. I don't know how good you are at learning foreign languages, but I think that's pretty fast. How was I able to do that? I attacked the language because I knew that in order for me to do the things I wanted, I needed to speak the language well, and I still wanted to be a writer. So even though I didn't have the confidence to yet write yet, I knew that the more I became acquainted with English, the quicker I would be able to develop the confidence to write books. (Spoiler alert: I graduated from college and eventually became a full-time writer. I am sucker for stories with a happy ending).

One of the subjects I hated growing up was math because I was told math was hard.

Have you been told by a parent or a relative or a teacher that math was hard, or that it's boring? My whole life all the way through high school and college, I struggled with math. I managed to pass my classes, just barely. I hated everything about it. Funnily enough when I was in college, I took statistics and I was really good at it. I was surprised by how much I liked it, even though it was math. I think it may have had something to do with the fact that statistics was more analytical, and we had to write reports about our findings.

My last corporate job was in purchasing, something I have always been good at it. Many island people are gifted at buying and bartering. Even though, I've been in the States longer than I lived in my native land, I will always be about getting the deal, sourcing and making sure that I am still an island girl at heart. I don't think that will ever change.

I got this job in purchasing and it was more strategic than I thought it would be. I told you that I was in IT & Telecom which meant that I sourced IT-related products and services. Let me give you an example, let's say that one of our member companies (I used to work for a coop) needed to buy 500 computers. Instead of just buying 500 computers, I would go to our other members and ask them if they needed to buy computers within the next 4-8 weeks. For the sake of this example, let's say five of them said they needed to buy computers also. I would collect all their specs (requirements) and pricing history and create a Master shopping list.

Then I would go to the market needing 3000 computers at the same time (instead of the original 500). That gave me more buying power because I would be spending more money. Yes, I would not be buying the same exact computer, but I would be placing a large order at the same time. Why was that important? Because vendors want revenue, they want a positive impact to their bottom line. That means I got the best pricing in exchange for a big purchase order. to give me better pricing, so they could get that big purchase order. Wow, I just got excited sharing that example with you. I can't believe how much sense this makes as I write it.

Why did I hate it so much when I was doing it then? Maybe I hated the politics or working in an office with people I did not like, or I just plain hated what I was buying. Anyway, I did that for four LONG years. I saved the company and its members a lot of money; millions of dollars in fact, but I hated it. Can you believe that I hated doing something that I was really good at? As much as I hated it, I was still good at it. Imagine if I had loved it? I would have probably saved them a fortune.

The whole time I kept praying that I would be released from the job. I was making six figures, I had 10-weeks of vacation time, and I worked five-miles from my house (probably even less). My schedule was very flexible. As a mom, from time to time I had to take my daughter to doctor's appointments, or if she had a day off from school, I could work from home. But still, with all of these perks, I hated the job because I was not buying anything that I cared about. I did not care for our members (we had to fight and push to save them money). I also felt like life was passing me by and I was not living my purpose. What I was not aware of was the fact that God did not release me from that job until I changed my mind about purchasing, strategic sourcing and math. God is funny like that.

Guess what? I began to look at numbers in a whole different way. I told myself, "You know what, fine. If I have to do this, I will do it well." I got really, really good at my job. And then I was immediately released from that job, just like that.

The Who

I began to ask myself who do I want to work with? I would love to tell you that I accepted the who right away, but I did not. I resisted because that's what I was told. I felt like a fraud, a liar and fragmented because I could not accept who I was called to serve. You probably have experienced something similar, have you?

When I FINALLY accepted that I was called to work with Kingdom women (and a few determined men) that were already established in ministry and were looking to break into the marketplace everything changed. I won't lie, it was very scary to type that and even scarier to say it. But when I did, I felt a HUGE weight lifted off my shoulders. Don't know who you are called to serve? Worry not, I will help you figure out your who in step one.

The What

I'm good at many things. How do I know? I made a list of all the things at which I was good.

And that's how I came up with the six-book series I'll be working on sometime in the future.

Can you think of some things you are good at? They

can be simple to you, just like teaching is simple to me. The funny thing is that this is hard for some people. I'm not bragging on myself. I'm saying this is *my easy*. You probably can do more complicated things than me. And they come really, really, really easy to you.

But this, this is my easy. Easy peasy strategy. Finishing projects is what I do. I can put courses and programs together like nobody's business. It took me two-and-half hours to write the outline of this book, to design the original cover and to set up the pre-sell page (more on that later). Then I worked on it some more. Then I kept adding more stuff, obviously. But the concept, the name, the subtitle, the cover, presale page, the promotion; yeah, all that took me just 2.5 hours.

The Who and The What: Who Are You Going to Sell To & What Are You Going to Teach?

Who are you going to sell this thing to? You must know that BEFORE you know what you are going to sell. How do you do that? You must ask yourself the following questions:

- What group of people do I feel called to?

- Who is the perfect audience for my skills and experience?

- What group of people do I already know how to reach?

- As a member of _____, why am I the PERFECT person to help them?

You **MUST** make a list of all the things you are good at. **Here's an example**:

- I'm good at math

- I'm good at strategic outsourcing

- I'm good at mentoring (coaching) people

- I know how to teach things
- I can pretty much teach anything

What are you good at? You could make a mental note; better yet, you should write it down. You can write your list here or inside the workbook. I highly recommend you get a journal/sturdy notebook JUST for this program. You should be able to easily come up with at least 15 things at which you are good. Have fun! IF you get stuck, ask someone that REALLY knows you. They'll tell you.

I am good at:

1.

2.

3.

4.

5.

6.

7.

8.

9.

10.

11.

12.

13.

14.

15.

People want to have the kind of life and resources you are having.

Have you seen the movie, "When Harry Met Sally?" There's a famous scene where the two protagonists are at a diner. It's pretty funny. In the scene, Meg Ryan's character is just being silly and proving a point to her friend, Harry. There's a lady sitting on the other side of the diner who famously tells the waitress, **"I want to have what she's having."** Go to the end of the manual for the link.

Can I tell you that there are people out there that want to experience the ease that you experience every time you do that thing you do so effortlessly? They do. They don't want to struggle anymore. Someone just asked me today, "Do you know how to do this? Like how do you make that? How do you do that?" And immediately, I thought of someone that does know how to do that task very well. I mean the person is a master at it. They work fast and do a fantastic job. Me on the other hand, could probably do it, but it would not get done as well and definitely NOT as fast.

People want to experience the ease you experience. Take for example when you have to perform a task from your to-do list – by the way I think to do lists are the best thing ever, but only when you are able to add that little checkbox at the end of every item. Imagine your never-ending to-do list, and all those tasks staring at you in the face with imaginary judging eyes. You know the lists I am talking about; 20+ complex tasks to be completed **in one day only**. Then five o'clock comes and you have completed just TWO tasks, if that.

Instead, imagine, writing a **strategic** to-do list, and having 80%, if not 100%, of your list completed at the end of your day, I'm telling you, you are going to become a completion junkie because it feels amazing-and-a-half to cross important tasks and items off your list. The people assigned to you are waiting and looking for what you know how to do, they too want to experience that kind of accomplishment. They want to have what you are having.

When I travel for business or pleasure, strangers usually compliment my outfits; it's the funniest thing. I find myself saying things like, "Oh thanks so much. I did not think about it much, I just put this stuff on." Without fail, the person just looks back in disbelief and continues to praise the shoes, jewelry and anything else they think it's cute.

Guess what? I often take that skill for granted. I know what to wear when I travel; exactly what shoes to wear, how to mix and match, and what piece of jewelry to wear so I can take a simple and casual outfit and make it totally fabulous. Often it does not take much - a change of hairstyle, jewelry or makeup usually does the trick. At times, I forget that I actually wrote a style guide for women of faith, **Styling Faith: The Complete Style Guide**. Not everyone knows how to do that. Oftentimes, it takes them forever to get ready. For me, it takes no time at all. I have a photographic memory. I remember when I wore what. So, if I attend a conference again, I make sure - especially if the same people are going to be in attendance – to not wear the same outfits again. Why? Because I don't want to be seen with the same outfit again. Yes, of course I repeat outfits, but not for a long time, and certainly NOT the same way I wore it before. I even remember what I brought, and what I wore without having to write it down either.

The Problem – What is the Pain They Are Experiencing?

Do you know that there are people sitting on the sidelines, not living their best life because they don't have YOUR normal? It's really sad when I think about it. I talk to people all the time and I hear their struggles. I would always think, "Wow, if I had a product ready that outlined my process or system they wouldn't be in this situation". "If I had an audio book, PDF, paperback, how-to book, whatever you want to call it, index cards, flashcards, whatever! If I had written down my process, they wouldn't be where they are today."

Think about something you don't know how to do right now, anything, maybe one of the things that I mentioned before. Maybe you don't know how to shop for yourself. You know what you like but when you go to the store you can't find it. That's a real issue MANY women struggle with.

Imagine if I hadn't written, **Styling Faith: The Complete Style Guide**. People buy that book all the time. It costs $38.00 on Amazon. It's over 300 pages long. Why? Because it has everything a woman would want or need to know about style, and then some. When people ask me about my style or about shopping, I don't have to reinvent the wheel, I just tell them to get the book. Many people that have read it told me that it was like having me with them when they go shopping. I even covered how to dress before going to the mall or outlet. You know what? It makes me feel really, really good to know that I took the time to put the book together.

What is one thing you know you are struggling with right now? What would happen if someone were to tell you, "Briefly read/watch this, and by the time you finish, you'll know exactly how to do that thing every single time. Perfectly. No mistakes." How would you feel about that? Would it change your life? Would it make your life easier? Would that change the quality of your life? Think about it.

I'm thinking right now about Thanksgiving and Christmas. That's when I usually bake at least two of my renowned pecan pies. I have a problem though; I don't know how to make pie crusts from scratch. I have tried. I have watched videos. The funny thing is that I can make very complicated gourmet food. I can make some really fancy pants stuff because I worked one-on-one with a chef for six months. And he taught me how to make pie crust. But it just didn't take, I don't know what happened. I just don't know how to make pie crusts from scratch.

What do I do? I do my best to buy the top pie crusts money can buy. But the dream is to make my pies crusts from scratch. Right now, somewhere in the world, there is someone that could go to their kitchen, set up their phone on a tripod and walk me through the process, slowly and step by step. The results? I could stop making awful pie crusts. They usually come out crumbly and tough. But if someone were to teach me, I could become an amazing pie crust maker. That would be amazing.

Somebody reading this manual is a perfect pie crusts maker and saying to themselves, "Making pie crusts is easy peasy; as easy as riding a bike." It may, in fact, be you. You are probably thinking, "You are telling me that people would pay me money if I grabbed my phone and recorded a step-by- step pie crust tutorial?" That is EXACTLY what I am saying, **I would pay for that**. Why? Because I need that in my life, like yesterday.

If you are reading this manual and want to show me how to make pie crusts, please know that I would probably kiss and hug you as well. Why? Because it would change my life. I want you to think about that story for a moment. What is that one thing, if you knew how to do it would change your life? You got it? That's exactly how the people waiting to learn your easy feel, as if they were dying for you to show them how to do YOUR easy. Some are LITERALLY dying. For some, their life would change or drastically improve.

Think about that next time you entertain the idea of not putting your product or service together. And maybe, like me, you won't be writing just one book. You might create many how-to books. What are how-to books? How to books are simple step-by-step guides or maps.

Give me anything and I'll show you how you can teach it and make money.

Have you seen the movie, My Big Fat Greek Wedding"? That movie came out in the early 2000s. It is so funny. The dad was obsessed with everything Greek. He thought Greece was the best thing since Pepsi. He would say, "Give me a word, any word, and I will show you that the root of the word is Greek." I'm that Greek dad. Give me anything that you know how to do. I'll show you how you can make money teaching it. I know what you are thinking. "Catherine, I am not as prolific or well-educated as you are. I haven't lived in other countries. I haven't learned other languages. I don't really know how to do much of anything. I'm a very simple person." All that might be true, but you are absolutely, positively wrong. **You know how to do many things**.

I am basically trying to create a teaching monster out of you. By the time I finish with you, you are going to want to record yourself or write a bunch of how-to books on about everything you know how to do.

Have you ever heard of the sites Udemy or Lynda? Those sites are littered with people that have created classes or courses out of what they know how to do. I want you to start changing your mind about the things you know how to do. In the next section, I'm going to share more examples; be warned, you might not believe me. "Catherine you must be lying. There is no way I could teach that and charge people to watch it or consume it" Yes, honey. Yes. I'm telling you. Anything you know how to do you can teach, and someone in the world will buy it. You create it once, and then you'll be able to sell it over and over again. You'll be able to sell it forever. But you have to widen your horizons first; open your mind to the realization that you are very smart. I'm going to prove that to you in the next section.

Example of Things You Can Teach

This is the moment you have been waiting for. You want to know how you can do exactly what I'm doing right now and make it sound so easy. Ready? Here we go.

What can you teach? Let's say you have a great job that you love. It's the perfect job. Do you know that there are people that don't know how to apply for a job? I'm not kidding. I have had conversations with my sister about people that want to get a job but don't even know where to begin – how to apply, the interviewing process, how to follow-up on a prospective position, or how to negotiate their contract. Forget about negotiating their benefits package.

If you have an amazing job that you love, that's your receipt right there. Remember, you have to have proof you know how to do that thing you are trying to teach others. Then you put a package together, a quick easy to follow how-to book with scripts/steps to take to land a great job. You will be helping new college graduates, international students, or people who have never received instruction on how to go about getting a job. You never know how high up the corporate ladder those students could move up in the world. Those can turn out to be great connections to have in the future. You can easily charge $100-$250 for such a course/guide per person.

Do you homeschool your kids? More and more parents are choosing to homeschool their kids but have no idea where to begin. Maybe you organized other local parents so the kids could learn different subjects from different parents – which of course would get the kids out of the house and would give the parents some extra time back – you could put all the forms together, how-to guide with all steps necessary for examinations, registration with the education department and even tips to keep the lessons fun. You guessed it, that can be a course too.

I provide even more examples in the audiobook, so make sure you listen to it.

By now you can tell that making a product does not require thousands of dollars or hours. Do not try to make a Hollywood production of your product either. And please do not over-complicate things. Keep it easy peasy and put your product out there (you can always update it later). People are waiting and they need to learn your easy, pronto.

THE FORMULA – STEP BY STEP

Now that you have seen the formula in action, we can start breaking down each step as you work on YOUR easy. Let's get started!

Step 1: Who and What do you want to teach?

a.   The Who

The who is just as important as the what. But how do you figure that out? I remember the time my first coach asked me who I wanted to work with. I had NO idea, but I did not want to tell her that, so I made a person up. It was not pretty because we built a solution based on someone, I had NO idea how to serve.

Before I get into the content, let me give you this quick hack: more often than not, your who is you! Mind blown yet? Let me explain better. Your who, more than likely, is a version of who you were, who you are now, or who you are becoming.

Let me tell you who I am called to serve and then you will have a chance to discover who you have been called to serve. Cool? Awesome.

My audience is Christian women who are already established in ministry, have a business idea or have started the business already but are struggling to make the kind of impact and money they know they can make.

Here's more information about my Avatar (the special person I am called and delighted to serve). Her name is Faith by the way.

Faith is:

45-55 years old	Stuck serving an audience that can't afford her
Has experienced some success already	
	Travels for ministry
Already invests in herself	Wants to grow her business
Married with kids	Works out
Divorced with kids	Takes care of herself
Into Fashion	Wants to pursue both biz & ministry
Masters or PhD degrees	
Drives a Mercedes Benz, Lexus, or MBW	Eats healthy
	Needs help niching down
Very busy	Needs help putting her program together
Into shoes, bags, and jewelry	
Reads & listens to books	Does not know what she should teach
Lives primarily in the south (United States)	
	Minority women
Grew up in church	

Disclaimer:

Faith is the combination of many versions of me; I know her VERY well and I can help her because I have been where she is now. I do work with people outside of this group, but when writing and creating content I keep Faith at the top of my mind.

Now that you have a better understanding of my avatar, let's build your avatar. Do not forget to pray BEFORE you complete the exercises to make sure you are hearing from God, and not deciding on your own and more than likely, choosing the easier avatar.

You can choose to complete this exercise in the workbook OR you can choose to do it in your own journal, Evernote (an online notebook) or designated notebook. How did I do it? I prayed, brainstormed on my journal and THEN I typed it on Evernote so I would have access to it ANYWHERE and EVERYWHERE.

Exercise:

My avatar is: (after you do this work, give him/her/them a first name and a global name. For example: Mary, Single moms.

How old?	What does she/he like?
Ethnicity?	What does she/he not like?
Where are they in their journey?	What kind of music do they listen to?
Married or single?	
Kids no kids?	What TV shows do they watch?
Where do they get their coffee?	How much money do they want to make?
Who is their favorite preacher?	
Who is their favorite singer?	Do they work out or want to work out?
Do they go to concerts?	
Where do they vacation?	What's their favorite movie(s)
Level of education?	Where did they grow up?
What kind of car do they drive?	How do they feel about Disney?
Do they live in an apt, condo or house?	Democrat or Republican?
	Do they love fashion?
Do they read?	Geographically, where do they live?
What kind of books do they read?	

Can you see how having this information will help you better connect with this avatar on social media through the copy you write or content you share? This is gold.

Who is my Avatar?

Name: _____ Global Name_____

_____

Ask yourself the questions in the previous page. As you go along you may come up with more questions that will further help you establish your perfect avatar. Write them down and use them as well. Ready, set, go.

_____

_____

_____

_____

_____

_____

_____

_____

_____

_____

_____

_____

_____

_____

_____

_____

_____

_____

_____

_____

_____

_____

_____

_____

What do you want to teach?

You have no idea how excited I am about teaching this portion of the formula? I mean I would even pay someone to let me do this. I'm getting paid for this work actually, but still this is how much I love it. How would you like to spend a day or a couple days teaching something? What would you like to be doing?

Imagine if somebody paid me to go to the beach and check out the waves? Can you imagine? Oh my God. I would be there in a heartbeat; I would get my bathing suit and everything on in a few seconds flat.

How do you want to spend your time? What are you passionate about? Did you go from being a carnivore like me eating meat with meat on the side, to a vegetarian? Many people don't know how to do that. They don't know how to make healthy meals. Or how to make the change. They don't know how to make the mindset shift. I did that. I made the switch in 2012. I probably would have made the switch earlier if I had known how to do it and had known all the benefits associated with it as well.

It won't take you long to put this together. Think about how you want to spend your time? Have fun writing it down in the exercise section. It's your first product or service. Notice that I'm planting the seed that you will use this manual over and over and over again. Especially since you also have the workbook; you can print it again and go through this exercise again. How cool is that?   So, take the time to determine, "What do I want to teach? What comes easy for me?"

It might be Quantum Physics. That's okay, if that is your easy. I can tell you that it is NOT my easy. Ask yourself, "How do I want to spend my time?" And, don't forget, it can be as simple as making English tea, or traveling. Have you ever been to England? I haven't been to England yet. But if you have, you can put a simple MP3 file (audio file) together called: "The 10 things every American traveler must know before going to London. #Boom. Or maybe your title it: Five Must Visit Places While in London." Or maybe: "The Top Places to Buy Gifts in London." This is just one example of how your passion for travel can become a product.

Are you seeing how simple this is? What do you want to teach? You get to decide. You get to decide what you want to teach.

Base on my experiences, where I have been, who I am called to serve, and what I am a totally awesome at, I would like to teach:

_____

_____

_____

_____

_____

_____

_____

_____

_____

_____

_____

_____

_____

_____

_____

_____

_____

_____

_____

_____

_____

Step 2: Your Story

You need to tell them who you are, and why you are the person to teach them. Let me say that this is a very important step.

Here are steps to follow to tell your story in a way that helps you connect with your audience in an authentic fashion.

1. Take your time

Break it down. This, however, does not mean you talk about yourself for 20 minutes straight without a plan or strategy. If you are going to talk, don't go on and on. Introduce yourself. Tell them why you wrote the book or created the course/program/video; keep it brief but relevant. Yes, you can tell them your story without giving unnecessary details. For example, you can tell them where you were born but you don't have to give them the name of the hospital, the temperature the day you were born and how many classmates you had in the first grade. However, you can tell how the conditions in your childhood shaped the kind of leader you became. Do you see the difference? Tell them your story, give details but make sure EVERY detail is necessary.

2. Don't forget to be vulnerable

Please don't tell them anything that has nothing to do with what you are teaching. Do tell them something that lets them know that you are human; that you know/ understand their pain and that you can relate to why it is hard for them.

3. Explain why you

Do they understand who you are? What in your past paints you as the mentor and teacher they are looking for? Literally make a list of all the things that have happened to you and choose the ones they need to hear. The experiences that show the real you; the human version of you, not the curated Instagram version of you.

4.   Use Your Words

Your audience needs to get to know you; your phrases, funny sayings and everyday words. Don't go the fake fancy pants route and start using SAT words you don't actually use in real life. Remember, keep it real. "Can they understand what I'm trying to tell them?"

When I first began to introduce people to the The Teach Your Easy concept, I took five days to break it down. My audience knew exactly what I was going to teach them. I broke it down. I showed them I knew what I was talking about. They knew what I was going to teach them because the description and the cover was very clear. If you begin to write your story and get stuck, don't worry. Listen to the audiobook and hear how I told my own story.

5.   Tell Them Why They Want It

Do they want it? Or do they need it? Do not be afraid to tell them why they want it and needed. How do you do that? You describe it. You tell them how their life is going to be better, faster, easier, funnier, safer when they have the thing you are making available to them. Does that make sense?

Exercise: Use the space below, workbook or a dedicated journal to complete this section.

Stop reading and take 15-minutes to write the following down:

1. Tell them who you are.

2. Explain what the product is

3. Make sure that they want it or need it by describing it to them (in such a way that is appealing and easy to understand).

_____

_____

_____

_____

_____

_____

_____

_____

_____

_____

_____

_____

_____

_____

_____

_____

_____

_____

_____

_____

_____

Step 3: What is the pain they are experiencing today?

I gave you a very detailed example of me not being able to make pie crusts and I told you how painful it was and how it took extra time because I needed to go to different stores to find the best and healthiest available pie crusts. I also told you that I really wanted to take my pie game to another level and that making my own pie crusts would certainly help me with that goal. Got it?

Hopefully, you too had to learn the thing you are trying to teach, so you can understand your Avatar's pain language. If you already know the thing you are trying to teach then ask somebody you know, or maybe your best friend, a few simple key questions than can guide how you help them through their pain points. For example, you can ask, "Do you know how to do X?" "How would your life change if you knew "_____"? How is your life harder now because you don't know how to make pie crust?"

Pro Tip:

Before you begin asking the questions, get their permission to record their answers (use your phone) or take mad notes. Why? Because they are about to unleash on you all the reasons why they need this thing. They are about to give you AMAZING copy (the words to use in your promotions, sales page, flyer, video, etc.) You are welcome!

Here is a quick and simple script you can use when approaching friends or strangers for help:

"Hi Janet, how are you? Can I ask you a couple of questions? It will only take five minutes tops. I know you don't know how to do your makeup. How does that make your life harder? Do you have to go to the mall every time you have a big event? Do you have to pay a professional make-up artist? Does that prevent you from going to events or livestreaming on social media? I am asking because I am putting a resource together for people that struggle putting make-up on.

Ask questions like that. You can be honest and tell them why you want to know. People are very helpful when they know you are not trying to sell them anything. Make sure you do not take too much of their time either. If you asked for five minutes ONLY take five minutes of their time. If they want to talk longer that's cool, but make it clear you are done collecting information from them when the five minutes are up.

Step 4: Your Receipts

Your receipts. Meaning your qualifications. What qualifies you to teach that stuff? Think about it. Did you go to school for it? Did your grandmother teach you? Are you known for this thing? Do you have a certification? Do you have experience? Have you been teaching people your whole entire life and now want to make it official?

What are your receipts? What are your accomplishments? Have you received awards? Take me, for example, I teach people how to write books and create content; I have written over 21-books (as of this printing). I am a number one best-selling author, have over 21-courses and programs.

What can you prove? Do you have testimonials from current or past clients or customers? That's very important. If you don't have testimonials you can ask for them. You could say something like: "Hey, remember when I helped you set up your new house when you moved? Will you mind answering these three questions for me? How hard was moving before I helped you? How much time and money did my assistance help you save? And how is your life easier because of it? That's it. Those are the questions. Go ahead and write them down on the workbook or journal.

Step 5: Outline the Process

This is my jam, my thing. Now you have seen my process. I gave you my formula and an outline – which I am breaking down for you right now. It makes sense, right? Because I wrote it down, read it, and went over it. I made sure that everything was done in order so I would not confuse you. You should do the same for your avatar/audience/customer/client, or however you want to call the people you have been called to serve.

The outline is a very high-level view of what you are going to teach. Your next steps are to:

- Write it out
- Then type it and
- Then organize it.

Go over your process. Using the pie crust example again, start by making a list of ALL the ingredients. If your recipe calls for a very specific type or brand of flour tell them where to find it (what stores typically carry it or websites). Why? That way your student can make sure they have all the ingredients before they start making the pie crust. List the ingredients in the order they are needed or will be used. Tell them what items need extra preparation ahead of time. Some people, due to allergies, will need to make substitutions; let them know what items they can use instead. That will get you brownie points for sure - those students would be more likely to buy future courses or programs from you.

Continue showing step-by-step the process to follow to make pie crust: the equipment they will need. List everything simply so a beginner could follow: proper equipment, mixing the ingredients, kneading the dough, putting it in the refrigerator and then quartering and working the dough. Don't assume your student knows all the steps and how to do them. Know your audience. If possible, give them pictures or screenshots of every step.

If you are creating a course for experienced bakers then you will probably explain things a little differently. The key is knowing your audience.

But more than likely, someone that is buying a course about how to make pie crusts needs ALL the help they can get.

If you make a mental list of your process you might forget some key steps. Write it down instead, even the small or inconsequential things. Then read your list out loud to make sure you did not forget anything, and it makes sense. If it is part of the process, it must be included in your process. Then you can go ahead and type it. As you do this, you will see places where to improve, remove, or move up or down the list; and that is good.

Does that make sense? The outline is everything.

To recap, see it in your head, write it down, walk through it, type it, reorganize it. Does that make sense? This step is the meat and potatoes, the bones of your program/course/book/audiobook/video or whatever resource you end up putting together for your audience. The outline is extremely important. I teach this in detail in my program, Mapping Your Million Dollar Story Workshop. Outlining a book looks a little different. I have a complete formula for that as well. But for now, I just broke down for you how you can effectively teach what you know and the importance of giving your students step-by-step instructions. Make sense? Awesome.

Step 6: The Vehicle – How are you going to teach it?

This manual was first created as an audiobook. Why? Because I knew I wanted to coach you. And I know that I can be very persuasive aka bossy. I knew you needed this quickly and I could not wait until the hardback manual was done. I knew eventually I would create an e-book, and then this hardback version you are holding. That worked for me because I'm a techie. I'm a nerd. I already told you that. If you rather write all this stuff out first, then knock yourself out and write it out. Your audience will eat it up. If you want to do video because doing video is easiest for you, then do that. If you want to do it cookbook style; where you have many pictures and very short descriptions, or paragraphs, go nuts. You want to create a PDF, PowerPoint or a live event? **Go ahead and do what works for you.**

If you already have an audience and want to do a live version of your program you could do that, record it, and then sell the replay. You can get immediate feedback so you could improve, add or make the product event better.

How are you going to teach it? Video? Audio? PDF? Printed e-book? Figure that out.

If you're going to teach people how to make a pie crust, I would suggest you probably do a video. Get one of those grip tripods from Amazon like this one: http://bit.ly/selfie-tripod. It allows you to place your phone horizontally, so the camera view is on your hands, and over whatever pots or instruments you are using. The tripod is under $20 (at least at the time of this printing). You can also do a search on Amazon for a cell phone holder stand for livestream/makeup to see other options that may be available.

Step 7: Teach, but don't overdo it

Teach each step thoroughly but do not beat a dead horse. That's what I have been doing; I've been teaching you; I'm going deep, but I'm not spending more than 10 minutes per section. Why? Because this is all you need to get started. Give your audience what they need to know at each step and continue moving through your material. Teach it, be thorough. Be generous. Keep it simple. Will you agree that I have been generous with my teaching? And I'm not even done yet. Would you agree that you have already gotten your money's worth from this manual? Time for the four Bs: 'Be generous. Be kind. Be funny. Be brief.'

PART II

This is where we will be diving deep into your product. Are you ready to create YOUR Easy!

Step 8. The Product Logistics

a.   Write a description that pops

This is imperative. You must write a description that pops and make people want to throw money at you. What does that mean? You have your outline. You know how you're going to distribute the product. How are you going to tell people about it? It's all about what you write and how you say it.

Let me read to you what I wrote about The Teach Your Easy Audiobook when it first came out in early August 2018:

Pre-order your audiobook copy of The Teach Your Easy Audiobook! It will change how you look at EVERYTHING you know how to do!

The Audiobook includes the following:

1. *The formula to Teach your Easy*

2. *Example of The Teach Your Easy Formula*

3. *Before you teach ask the following questions:*

   Do they know me?

   Do they understand what it is?

   Do they want/need it?

4. *A sample list of VERY easy things you could be teaching and monetizing.*

5. *What is monetization and how to do it right*

6. *Don't complicate it, KISS - Keep It Simple Sweetie*

7. *When to start Teaching Your Easy: Now*

8. *Putting it all together*

9. *And More Nuggets to Help You Become a Master Teacher and Salesperson.*

The Audiobook will be ready on August 17th, or earlier.

Can't wait till then to get started? You can watch the Teach Your Easy five lessons I created here: http://bit.ly/tye-playlist

Does that make sense? I gave them everything they needed to make a purchasing decision. I kept it very simple. But I told them all the things they wanted and then I gave them even more stuff. The description does not have to be long, but it has to be clear. It has to be easily understood. It has to make sense.

Here's another example of copy I wrote for the audiobook: http://writingmadesimple.today/teach-your-easy/. This is called a Sales letter. You do not have to write or put something together that is this long, but I wanted to give you another example.

Exercise: Stop reading or listening to the audiobook and write your product's description right now.

_____

_____

_____

_____

_____

_____

_____

_____

_____

_____

_____

_____

_____

_____

_____

_____

_____

_____

It would be amazing if by the time you finish reading this manual you had your product completed. How cool would that be? I think it would be really amazing.

b. Create an image that pops

If you don't know how to design images, hire someone. Here's a referral for the person that designed the final manual cover: **https://www.imallisondenise.com/** Tell her I sent you.

I have an amazing series of videos where I show my students all my tricks and how to put things together, but for now, I will tell you that you can create the image yourself using a whole bunch of FREE resources like www.canva.com. They have a paid version of the platform, but for now the free version will work fine for you. They have many templates and you can go to town depending on what you want to create. I have a tutorial inside the series showing how I created the image for The Teach Your Easy audiobook. Plus, I also put together another book cover on camera. If I can do it, anyone can do it. If you don't know how to use Canva you can ask my cousin, YouTube, to show you how.

If you know that you are not going to be good at it because that's just not your forte, then hire somebody. There are sites like www.Fiverr.com where you could get a decent cover or image for about $15-$50 – depending on the designer and the caliber of the image you want. The investment is totally worth it, if you don't know how to do it yourself.

On the other hand, if you can do it yourself, which is what I did, save the money and invest it in something else. I didn't spend hours and hours putting the cover together either. Maybe an hour, tops. **I don't want you to spend hours upon hours putting something together either.**

Pro Tip:

Notice how I did not spend money to put the first audiobook together. I DYI'd the whole thing first. Then I got paid, and **then** when I saw it was something people wanted, I got a professional cover done and took the time to put a workbook together. Then I worked on this manual. Finally, I re-recorded a cleaner, and more organized version of the formula. But first I got paid and proved the concept.

I hope that makes sense. Please create that image. But if you don't know how to create the image, please, please, please, with sugar on top, hire somebody and get that product to market ASAP.

c.   What's the Upgrade?

This section right here is going to blow your mind wide open. Are you ready? What's the upgrade? Just earlier I mentioned Canva and I said that is easy to use. However, some people need to see step-by-step how to it should be used. So, I realized that many of the resources for some people are new. I decided to make it easier by doing screen shares of everything that I create. Why? Because some people will hear this once, they will understand and/or are familiar with the platforms I mentioned, and they'll get it done in no time. They're all set. However, there are other people that are going to need to see me do it. They tried to find www.canva.com and they couldn't find it. There's no shame in that; I'm anticipating that. They would probably say, "Catherine How do I do it? How do I know that I can do it? What size do I choose based on my product? Help!"

For these students, I created a more in-depth series of videos. Because some people are gonna need more hand-holding.

I created them ahead of time before I even started selling the audiobook. Why? Because I knew there was going to be a need and that, ladies and gents, is my upgrade. What does that mean? Simply put, I make more money but more importantly, at the end of the day, I'm helping more people.

There is a need and I have the solution.

So how can you help your audience? I want you to think about that. "How can I make their life easier?" Think intimacy = less people. What I mean by that is the more time they get to spend with you, the deeper you go in; that should cost more. Don't feel that you have to give everything away the first time around for a very introductory rate. You don't have to do that.

When I was teaching this, there were people that took action right away. I'm talking from the first day I did the live stream. However, there are other people that need to hear the information several times so, you give them the resources, you tell them how to do it and they are fine. There's another group of people that need more information. They need to see it, they need to talk to you, they need more, and there's nothing wrong with that. But because they need more, that costs more, it just does. I want you to become used to that. I want you to open your mind to charging more.

It's like when you take your car for an oil change. They tell you how much it is for an oil change. Then they go down the list - if you want to change your windshield wipers, there's a cost for that. If you want to have your tires rotated, that is extra. If you want to have your transmission fluid flushed and replaced, you guessed it, that's extra. But what you initially needed was just the oil change. They'll do that for $30 bucks or whatever it costs. Anything above that is going to cost you more.

Does that make sense? It's very important that you realize that you always have to anticipate the next level of help your Avatar will need and how you can supply that need. But do not forget how you can increase your revenue. Does that make sense?

Exercise:

Read this section and at the end you will see a section to complete this exercise. I want you to think for five minutes or so, of the next level of what you are teaching. Figure out what your upgrade is going to be. It doesn't have to be complicated or cost a lot either. Just think about the next logical step or concept your ideal client needs in their journey.

For example, let's keep the pie crust example. You created that course for me (I really hope somebody does). I finally learned how to make pie crusts that are delicious, buttery and flaky. Then one day you send me an email that says, *"Catherine your pie crusts are coming out unbelievably, right? Since you learned to make pie crusts your pie game got elevated to a whole new level. But do you know how to decorate your pie crusts?"*

You know what I am talking about? You have probably seen on the Food Network how Ina Garten or other bakers, they make cut outs out of dough and then make little leaves and even season appropriate designs. Of course, you are going to have leftover dough. Wouldn't you love to learn how to decorate pie crusts?

Why would I think that's included in the initial pie crust making course? I can totally see myself saying, *"Oh, for an extra $25-$40 bucks I can upgrade to that option? Yes, please. I want it."* However, if I don't want it, I can just say no. Do you see how you would be helping me? I don't want you to see upgrades as just a way to make more money. It is another way to make your customer's life easier and to add value.

I'm trying to expand your mind. Because many experts like to give stuff away. Stop doing that. Everywhere you go to buy stuff they charge you for it, don't they? When you go to Qdoba and they're making your burrito and you ask for extra guacamole they don't give it to you for free. They'll give it to you alright, but they'll charge you extra.

Guacamole always cost more; avocado always cost more. You understand what I'm saying? There is value in what you know. There is value in what you know. There is value in what you know. Got it? Good.

Exercise: What is the next level of this thing I'm teaching?

_____

_____

_____

_____

_____

_____

_____

_____

_____

_____

_____

_____

_____

_____

_____

_____

_____

_____

_____

_____

_____

_____

_____

_____

_____

d. Setup the Pre-Sale

Grab your pen and your paper because your presale period is very important.

How are you going to make money? Do you have a payment processing account like PayPal? If you don't have one, go to www.paypal.com and set one up. It's free. It's awesome. You can setup your presale with PayPal. There are many other sites that you can use. The one that I use if you were paying attention is www.Moonclerk.com It's not free. However, to me, it is worth every penny. It is very easy to use. You can attach a description and an image of your product as you can see here: http://bit.ly/teachyoureasycourse, and also setup reoccurring payments as well.

If you end up creating a program, such as a gardening or cooking series, you can charge every month or every week. You can do that with www.PayPal.com but I feel that with Moonclerk it's just a little more fancy pants, and it's super easy to setup. You can do so many things with Moonclerk but, again, it is not mandatory that you use it. For those of you reading this manual and you decide to use Moonclerk, I have a video series in which I discuss how I use the platform, how I set up my forms, how I add pictures, how I setup the emails inside Moonclerk so I don't have to spend time welcoming people to my programs one at a time.

Pricing:

You have setup the payment button, how much are you going to charge? Let's quickly talk about it. Let's say you're not sure, because you have not sold anything before and you're not sure how much to charge.

The easiest way to figure out what to charge for your product, e-book, service or course is to see what the competition is doing. Do some research and find out what others are charging for something similar.

If you're teaching something like a book or program like this, you could setup a pre-order price. I would even add some bonuses. You could also just offer that introductory rate for a limited amount of time. That would motivate people to move quickly and purchase your product before the price goes up.

You can decide how much you want to make. Let's say that you're doing something for free now before turning it into a program. Maybe you decide to create *The Easiest Way to Make Pie Crusts From Scratch Course*. I would easily pay $30 for that step-by-step video. Seriously, you know how often I make pecan pies? I am also thinking about my delicious apple crostatas; they are amazing.

I want you to think about the lifetime value of what you're selling. This manual, for example, or the audiobook, you're going to be able to use this over and over again. When I give you the workbook, you're going to be able to print it over and over again. Go through the sections, fill it out and make another product and another product. How many times are you going to do that? There is no limit, right?

Think about the value, the lifetime value of your product? How often are they going to use this thing? Muy importante, right? So, think about that. Now that you know what is included in this program would you pay $497for this? How much money is this going to make you over your lifetime? It's already worth $99. Especially with all the resources that I'm teaching and all these strategies, right?

Create a pay button, charge $30 - $50. You can even charge $9.99 at first and then raise the price later. Please charge more money. Create a button, come up with a release date and launch it.

What do I mean by come up with a release date? I knew that I would deliver this product quickly. I knew that it would not take me long to produce this. When I pre-sold the audiobook on day one, I said coming soon; I did not even give an actual date. On the following day I said it would be released in less than 30 days. I gave an actual date because I know me. I know what I can do, and I know my work ethic. Please know thyself and come up with a realistic release date for your products. (always keeping your current commitments in mind). People pay. Just know thyself. How long is it going to take you?

But it is VERY important that you remember this: you don't have to wait until your product or service is completed to make money.

That's the presale step, you come up with how much you're going to charge, create a payment button on PayPal, Moonclerk, Sam Cart, Kajabi, etc. Then release the presale. Pre, meaning it is not created yet, but you still are going to make some moola once you let the world know about it.

e. Promote, Promote, Promote

This is where you have to come out of your shy shell. This is when you have to get out there and hustle. You have to let people know what you have created for THEM. It is not for you to JUST make money. You MUST remember this thing you have created will change their lives in a dramatic and awesome way.

If you want to follow the way I do it you are more than welcome to. Why? Because it works very well. It worked for me! Give yourself enough time to build curiosity, educate and let people get familiar with you and your fantastic offer.

Take some time to educate and promote; three or five days should work, but if you are just getting started on social media you should give yourself more time. I did take five days to teach something I was already covering in the program/manual. Why? Because I already have a social media following and people know who I am. The initial cost of the audiobook was low, so it did not take a lot of convincing. The higher the cost of your program the more intentional you have to be about promoting and sharing on social media and/or email (if you have an email list already).

Teach broadly on the subject for a number of days. At the end, tell them how to preorder. If you want to know what I'm talking about and want to see how I did it, you can go to: www.bit.ly/teachyoureasy-playlist That is a free playlist of the five days I taught live. I taught and I gave, and I gave, and I gave, but you better believe that every time I finished, I told them where to get more information. I told them I could help them even more.

Do you see what I mean? I gave first; I added value. I did not stop there. I also promoted everywhere throughout the day: wherever I had a presence on Facebook - my group and pages; on Instagram, YouTube, Pinterest, LinkedIn, Twitter, and any other platform available. I created the product, but I didn't just let it be. I shared it. And I shared it. And I shared it. You get it? Are you with me? That's what I mean by promote, promote, promote.

You cannot overdo it. Why? Because you're giving and adding value. The way social media platforms algorithms are these days you have to share your content many times so people see it. You have to share many times so people know what you're talking about. You have to share many times so the person that didn't see it or missed at 1pm can see it at 3pm.

It's very, very important that you follow this formula so you can give your program more chances to succeed. The success of your program, your resource, or how-to book is very much dependent on how much you serve and how much you promote.

You found this manual and program because I promoted it. It is that simple. Remember the quote from the movie, "Field of Dreams", "Build it and they will come"? Well, yes, you have to build it first, but you also have to **tell** them. And THEN, they will come.

If you want to know how I did it, you can follow me on social media under Catherine Storing and see how I share my programs. This year I decided to teach a new training EVERY week. All people have to do is register for it. You can check it out here: http://bit.ly/buildwealth-webinar. It's great because I am adding value and building my email list at the same time. I am committed to doing 52-intentional teachings in one year. At the end of year, I will have a robust program I can either sell or use as bonus for a program. Even though this is a FREE training, it is a product nevertheless, and it requires consistent promotion and sharing.

When I re-share my livestreams or post on social media, I just don't hit the share button and that's it. That's spammy. Instead I come up with a quick sentence, or quote that invites my audience to watch or consume my content. Something like, "Do you need to make more money?" Or "Do you know how to teach what comes naturally to you? No? Then you need to watch this…"

I literally did that several times a day, for five days straight.

Then I did story time (what I call my livestreams). One of the most popular ones, "Do you even know who you are? Let me remind you." I shared that over and over again. But I added value every single time. The name of the game is: promote, promote, promote. Got it?

Where are you going to promote? Maybe you don't want to be in all the platforms at the same time. That's totally okay. You may want to be on Facebook or maybe your people are on Instagram, so you'll talk to them there. Are you with me? Pick a place, and if you can, plaster it everywhere. Don't know how to do it? Ask somebody for help; hire somebody. Hire your teenager.

You can also schedule your posts ahead of time. Whatever it is that you need to do, please, get it done. Inside the Teach Your Easy video series I will show you step-by-step how I schedule my posts using tools like www. buffer.com They have a free version I use, and it is very easy to setup. The other free tool is www.hootsuite.com. You can schedule the posts ahead of time and that way you don't have post all the time. Take one Saturday morning, write all your posts - and again, if you want to cheat you can look at my Facebook page: https://www.facebook. com/catherinestoring/, then take a couple of hours in the afternoon to schedule everything. Easy peasy. It is all about communicating, adding value and driving them to a page where they can learn more and buy your stuff.

Please understand, I am not saying to tell people, "Buy my stuff." I never ever want to see you doing that. Try a post like this one:

"Do you love making pies but don't know how to make your crusts from scratch? I know you're tired of going through the process only to end up buying frozen crusts. Guess what? I have put together an easy to follow program, "Five Simple Steps to Make the Most Delicious, and Flaky Homemade Crusts". Click here to find how it works."

You see how easy that was? It does not have to be complicated. Simple works EVERY time.

There's another tool I want to share with you, www. Bitly.com. Please don't go online sharing long and ugly links. How do you think I have been sharing easy to remember URLs? I use Bitly! The platform also provides great analytics; it lets you know how many people have clicked on your link and on what days. Very helpful information to have when you are promoting a free training or paid program. For the Pie crust making program you could create a link following the below example (if it is available of course), bit. ly/easypiecrusts. I hope that makes sense. Don't forget: promote, promote, promote.

f. Ask Questions and pay attention - What is your avatar complaining about?

I told you that I took five days to tell people and taught them about Teach Your Easy. I taught, and while I was teaching people were posting, commenting and they were telling me what was hard for them. Guess what? I was paying attention. I would go back to my livestream post and I would read what they wrote. They would ask great questions. I was paying attention because often what they were asking seemed so simple or basic to me that I forgot to mention or did not think to add to my manual or program. Why? Because it was SO easy for me, but it was not for them. But because I asked questions, because I added value and I paid attention I was able to add more content to the program.

The pre-sale process is two-fold, it allows you to make money right away and it also helps you make the program/course/book or e-Book better. You heard that? You make money, you learn what else they need from you and then you add it. Basically, they are helping you create a better product.

Does that make sense? Ask questions. Pay attention and ask questions. That's why you are adding value because you want to create a really good product for your avatar. You better believe that there were some things that I had to add because I didn't even think about it. Take advantage of the pre-sale process. It is your best friend when it comes to creating content for the solution your client is looking for.

g. Add/Tweak to your product or process as you see fit

Once you have paid attention and asked those questions from your audience, go back and add the new content in the right places. Don't just add it all randomly. Add the new content where it will help your customer the most. By the way, don't be afraid to add more. Don't be afraid to give more either. If it makes sense, be generous. Are you with me? Be generous.

Step 9: Create the Product

Keep it simple, though. What do I mean by that? If you're going to create an e-Book, write it on Microsoft Word. When you've finished writing, click on save as and select PDF, then save the file. You're done. I'm hoping you know how to use Word, but if you don't know, you can ask either of my cousins Google or YouTube. They'll tell you how to use it. Most people know how to use Word. If you are a Mac person like me, you can use Pages – Apple's version of Microsoft Word.

If you're going to create an audio program, you can use your phone to record it. If you have an iPhone (the best) you can use the Voice Record app: http://bit.ly/voicerecordapp If you have an Android phone, that's okay, I still love you. They also have a similar app.

If your product is a T-shirt, I can help you with that too. Maybe you come up with great quotes, but you don't want to incur the expense of printing and then shipping shirts all over the country or world. If that is the case, I have a resource for you: https://teespring.com/ Why? Because you don't have to print shirts ahead of time or buy them either. People buy them and you get paid. A t-shirt can be the upgrade for your Making Pie Crusts Program. You can see a live T-Shirt Campaign here: http://bit.ly/watchme-work

For example, I came up with an idea for shirts for the new year. I did not print a whole bunch of shirts BEFORE I knew whether or not people would buy it. No, first I created a campaign and ordered one shirt for me and another for a friend. Then when I was ready, my friend and I would wear the shirt to promote them. I get paid if people purchase the shirts. There is no risk for me since I bought the printed shirt at cost. So, even if no one buys the shirts I will still have a pretty looking shirt. How cool is that? Make sure you are following me on Instagram so you can see that cool shirt: https://www.instagram.com/catherinestoring

a.   Deliver the Product

You have created a digital product, the e-Book I suggested you create, but how do you deliver it? Listen up: https://payhip.com/. It is a great way to deliver the product, and to get paid as well. There's no recurring fee other than the transaction fee after someone buys your product. Do your due diligence and find out what those fees are here: https://payhip.com/pricing

The other platform which I like a little better – this is for advanced course or content creators – is https://warriorplus.com/. This platform also allows you to deliver your content, but more importantly, it allows other people to find your product, and sell it for you. You have to give them a commission, but only if the product sells. Again, this is a little more advanced but if you continue to learn about courses or decide to attend the next The Teach Your Easy Virtual Retreat you will see the step-by-step tutorial I created. What I love the most about Warrior Plus is that you create the product, other people sell it and get to make money as well. Win-win for everybody.

Let me recap: you create a PDF. You upload it to Warrior Plus and you charge $15 for it. There are people out there that don't want to create products, but still want to make money. They are looking for great products to promote. While they are looking for a cool product, they see product about Making Pie Crusts. They say, "Wow, that program looks really cool. I would like to sell it for them. How much will the creator give me to sell it for them?" – The commission percentage is decided and setup by you at the time you are putting your page together on Warrior Plus - since it cost you zero dollars to create the product you probably would not mind giving away 40% or 50% commission to your 'sales person'.

The sale person loves the deal, goes to town selling the product for you like hot cakes and then Warrior Plus gives you the balance of the sale - after the sales person gets paid. You can read more about their program here: https://warriorplus.com/features

Now you can see why I said this platform was for advanced creators, right? Don't start with this one, use PayPal or Payhip to get started, make some money, and then pay someone else to setup Warrior Plus for you (that's what I did when I tried setting it up years ago. Best money I ever spent).

Once you finish putting your product together you must deliver on the promise. Send them an email with instructions on how to access or download their product. You must deliver the product otherwise you're going to get chargebacks (when people contact their bank or credit card company because you did not do what you promised you would do). Also, even if they don't contact their bank or ask you for a refund, they will never buy anything from you and will tell all their friends on social media to never buy anything from you. And that my friend, would not be so good for you or your business.

You have to deliver your product when you said you were going to deliver it. But if some reason life happens (meaning you or your child get sick or something prevents you from delivering on time) you must tell them,

> *"I'm so VERY sorry. It will be another week until you receive your product. However, I will add such and such bonus (add a tutorial, extra training, something that will make their life easier) just because of the inconvenience."*

You got it? Be honest and be generous. People will forgive you and will remember how generous you were. Do you see how I'm giving you more than I promised? You already are in the plus; it doesn't cost me extra to be generous? Be generous.

Step 10: Keep Promoting (advanced)

If you have the budget take advantage of paid traffic, I would recommend that you actually - this is advanced - don't use this at first – Why? Because this comes out of your own pocket. You can waste a lot of money if you don't know what you are doing. Still, I have a strategy which you can use when you are ready, and after you have a system in place, e.g., after your book is selling.

Remember, I created that FREE YouTube playlist, right? Well, I'm going to take the playlist on YouTube and set it up on https://mailchimp.com/ (an amazing email marketing platform for beginners). I will show how to use it. I'm going to offer the YouTube playlist on Facebook or Instagram (using Facebook Ads) in exchange for their email address (this is an excellent way to build my email lists by the way). Why would I want to do that? Because then I can encourage them with more value and resources. Not only for this but future product as well.

Once they receive the playlist and follow-up emails, I will send them the link to buy my program, and then my retreat or anything else that will help them in their content creation journey. Boom. Done. More money for me. Get it? You can do the same thing, if you have the budget and if you know what you're doing.

If you don't know what you're doing, you hire somebody to do the Facebook or advertising ads for you. Is not hard but you MUST know what you're doing so you don't overspend or fall flat on your face. If you don't know how to use Facebook ads, seek out a friend that does or hire someone if you can afford to do so. Either way you now have this strategy to use when you are ready. Next time you have a baby girl you might just name here Catherine or Cat out of gratitude ☺ I am just kidding…sort of.

That's how you create your product. You are going to kill it out there. I just gave you all my tips.

Again, you can also create really pretty, PDF products for free on Canva. Let me give you an example of one I put together myself, go to: http://bit.ly/wybi90days-guide. How cool is that? You now know how to put your product together and even how to deliver it.

a.   Promote on autopilot – advanced

Using either Buffer of Hootsuite (or any other post scheduling tool) to continue sharing the same posts that you wrote before and the same videos you used before on social media so you can continue to make money on a regular basis.

One of my favorite things to see when I walk into my home office in the morning and open my email inbox is sales notifications. While I was sleeping someone bought something I created once, and I keep getting paid. It's like printing money basically.

PART III

Now that we have gone over the ENTIRE 10-Step Formula to Teach Your Easy, let's continue on this journey so you can better comprehend, implement, assimilate, and continue using this formula in your business.

MORE EXAMPLES OF THINGS YOU CAN TEACH

I know I already gave you a few ideas of what you can teach but I wanted to give you a few more. You are welcome!

You are probably reading this book right now and thinking about how easy it is for you to put together resumes. You are a master resume builder. Your resumes are masterpieces – think and the Michelangelo's David sculpture. I bet you can whip up resumes in no time. I remember the time I paid someone to put my resume together. She charged me $500 and I gladly paid it. You could create a screenshare product or course and charge $100.00 for it. This is a bonus idea for you. You are welcome!

You can put your resume inside your course or program as an example. This is a great move because those people are going to get jobs and they are going to have access to your resume. If they ever feel that they have an amazing position that matches your qualifications, they are going to call you. How? They would have easy access to your contact information. You are welcome.

Let's say you know how to setup 503(c) organizations. You could put together a quick questionnaire, find the forms for each state, and a quick video lesson on completing the forms. That program would probably sell itself. Many people in ministry that want their own foundation would love to know how to get started. Talk about your own journey and the mistakes you wish you had not made.

Here's another - maybe you are part of a multi-level marketing company – like Avon, Mary Kay, essential oils, wraps, etc., and have done very well with the company. You could put together a how to grow your team or how to really connect with people without being annoying – like sending out the blue DMs (Direct Messages).

Do you know how to buy a car; the benefits of leasing versus owning? What about car ratings, American versus foreign cars? Create a course. That course would help SO many people.

Are you great at buying groceries? Do you know how many people don't know how to buy groceries? They have no idea what items to buy in bulk and what items to buy every week. They don't know where to find coupons or how to use them. Some people think they have to buy ALL their groceries in just one store. I am telling you, you could be helping people save money and eat better at the same time.

Did you get married on a budget and yet still had a lovely party? Did people have a blast. What if you put a list of the top wedding websites, wedding gown stores or designers, wedding magazines or questions to ask venue managers or caterers? Many brides and parents would love to have a wedding planning one-stop shop course or place to find ALL the wedding answers they need.

HOW TO MAKE MONEY – THE THING YOU DID NOT LEARN AT CHURCH, BUSINESS SCHOOL, OR FROM BOOKS ABOUT MONEY

Stop Being Broke and Monetize Your "Normal"
– Catherine E. Storing (What does that even mean?)

Where is the money? In other people's wallets. I am sorry if you were expecting some deep answer. The truth is that if you want to make money without having a J.O.B (just over broke) you must exchange something of value for their money.

"But what if I hate selling and asking people for money, Catherine?" Great, I can help you with that. The reason why you hate selling is because you think you are asking for money. Am I right? The reality is that if you follow the 10-Step Formula to Teach Your Easy you would actually be offering the solution someone has been praying for. Do you see the difference?

You probably think selling is a four-letter word because you keep picturing a sleazy used-car salesman. That is NOT you, at all. You are an anointed, blessed and experienced solution deliverer. If I am right, you are more than ready to over deliver on your promise, am I right? How do I know? Easy, I over-deliver ALL the time. Why? Because I HATE, yep, I said hate, when people under-deliver to me. My solution is to lead by example. I deliver WAY more than I promise so when my students learn from me, they too become over-deliverers, thus flooding the world with people that LOVE to give.

Why do you think Jesus said in Acts 20:35 that it is better to give than to receive? Because the feeling you experience when you give more than you receive is almost indescribable. Try it sometime.

Going back to looking at sales the right way... **When you provide a solution for which people are grateful, they are MORE than happy to give you their money. What am I saying? You are NOT in the sales business, you are in the solutions business.** Doesn't that feel much better? Whenever someone reaches out to me for help with business strategy or content, I don't feel apprehensive or upset, I get happy. Why? Because I KNOW I was created to help others monetize their easy. Imagine if I did not feel comfortable charging you for this manual? I would not be able to continue printing it because I would run out of money in no time.

Instead, I am MORE than happy to tell you about this manual because I know I jam packed it with ALL the tools (did you see how many resources I shared with you? 37. Yeap, I counted them. (Check the resource page at the end of the manual for ALL the links). You get to make a difference in the lives of the people YOU have been called to serve.

How do you feel about sales now compared to before your reading this section? I hope you are more than enthusiastic about presenting your solution(s) to the people you have been called to serve. Why did I add that last part? Because if you were to offer the wrong solution to the wrong person it just would not work. Let me explain better with a story.

Years ago, I lived in Concord, NH. There was a local Mexican restaurant I used to love to go to after work on Fridays. One of those Fridays some entertainment company came to the restaurant to run a trivia game. Since I was already there, and I am SUPER competitive I decided to play, and I won one of the categories. The prize the MC chose to give me (remember, I was living in Concord, NH and this was the dead of winter), was FREE tanning lessons. I, an island girl, won FREE tanning lessons. Even though I was happy to win I was NOT happy about winning tanning lessons. Yes, it was the dead of winter, but I already have home-made tanned skin. I gave the FREE tanning sessions away and did not participate on the trivia games again.

They lost me because they tried to "sell" me the wrong thing. The MC saw me give away the tanning sessions certificate to someone in the audience (that was not very nice of me, but that's how disappointed I was). Make sure you follow step 1 and take the time to learn who you are called to serve and just sell to those people. Got it? I hope so.

DON'T COMPLICATE IT – KISS:
KEEP IT SIMPLE, SWEETIE

I can almost see you thinking about VERY innovative and TOTALLY outside of the box ways to Teach Your Easy. You are probably dusting off your drawing instruments or building tools so you can create something amazing. Please STOP. Do not be that person. DO NOT try to be a wheel inventor. The wheel has been invented already. This is not the time to try to do something so far out (do people still say that?) that it would take you months or even years to create your thing only to discover that people don't even want to buy the thing you created or understand how it works.

KISS – Keep It Simple Sweetie (this is my clean and much nicer version). Easy does it. Be innovative in the way you interact with your audience, how you teach and how you show up, but DO NOT, I repeat, DO NOT trip yourself up by trying to put together a course, program or service that is TOO hard or complicated. Your audience needs simple, and so do you.

Think about your favorite book, product, movie or provider. Do they make it easy or hard for you to work with them and give them money? Not hard at all, right? Then, please do yourself and your audience a favor and make the process super easy and fun for them.

THE TIME TO TAKE ACTION
IS NOW

a.   Do the Work

I bet you can tell I am setting you up with that question, right? The PERFECT time to put together YOUR Easy and telling the world about it is RIGHT NOW! Not when the kids go to college, when you lose those last 10lbs, when things slow down at work or church. Nope, the time is RIGHT NOW. There will NEVER be a better time to come out of the shadows and take your spot in the center of the stage of your calling.

Can you see yourself? Ready, nervous, excited, and full of expectation? I can. You look amazing. You have been built for this day, but the show cannot start if you don't take your spot. It is time for you to say yes. Will your voice shake? Absolutely. Will you mess up your lines? More than likely. Will some people not get it at all? Yeah, that is VERY likely. Will you be stretched in ways you have not experienced before? You got it. BUT, and this a VERY big but, you WILL NEVER regret getting started now; however, you will regret waiting. I can tell you from experience that I wish I had not procrastinated for so many years. It is one of the many reasons why I go hard. I'm making up for lost time.

Don't be like me. Take the center stage and take the bull by the horns (or whatever softer and gentler metaphor you would like to use) and show it who's boss. You were created for this; there are often lives on the balance. Be like Michael Jordan and just do it.

b.   Accountability – What it is, why you need it, and how to get it

I have long been acquainted with accountability. A coach introduced me to it which changed my life.

Accountability is like having a big sister that walks the hard and uncharted waters with you. Find someone that is as committed and excited to create, give and grow with you. Someone that believes in you and your calling. DO NOT choose someone that accepts your half-baked excuses or babies you when you flake for the 10th time. You need a drill sergeant meets your favorite aunt. I bet you are already thinking of someone, aren't you?

HOW TO SHARE YOUR PRODUCT – MARKETING: RELATIONSHIP BUILDING

In steps 8 and 10, I covered sales so why am I doing it again here? Because it is THAT important. The thing is sales and relationship building are completely different, but then again not really. Let me explain. If you want to make cash fast you might want to concentrate on a quick marketing strategy but if you want to grow your business, brand and platform then you must consider building a relationship with your audience. But how does one do that? I am glad you ask.

Have you seen big social media influencers and what they post online? They don't just post the products and brands they represent; no, they also show you glimpses of their lives and moments where they are human. Like the time their face broke out with pimples, or they got themselves locked out of their car/house, or when they overslept and missed their flight. Why do you think they do that? Because people are interested in people. Imagine if you show up on social media always looking all put together and perfect, everything in its place and always working out. How fun is that? Imagine if all the reality shows on TV were like that? They would not last more than one season, if that. If you look at any of the plots of those shows, there is always a crisis brewing or a fight about to happen. Why? Because people want to see real life. Now I am NOT suggesting you turn your life into an episode of the Kardashians, but I am suggesting you begin to share more of your life, going to get coffee at Starbucks, working out, picking up your kids form school, complaining about the long wait at the store. Real life stuff. If all you do is post business stuff about your products and services your audience will feel like they are being sold to, and NOBODY wants to be sold to.

There are a few social media influencers I am following right now, and I LOVE when they post pictures of their kids and/or their home; or when they go live, and their house is a mess, or they are sick. Somehow knowing they get colds and have fights with their kids makes me like them even more.

Talk to your audience about your wins and your products but not all the time. Ask them how they are doing, engage with them. Give them gifts JUST because. I love when I receive just because gifts. It makes me feel appreciated. Your audience is NO different. They want to feel appreciated too. Once in a while, give them something they want from you. How would you know that? Listen, ask questions, and never stop getting to know them. If you listen carefully enough, they will tell you EVERYTHING you need to know.

Be intentional about your posts, videos and marketing. Always have your audience and their needs in mind and watch how your numbers, bank account and more importantly, your impact grow.

WHAT'S AVAILABLE TO YOU

Now that you know how To Teach Your Easy (after I gave you and taught you all these strategies and resources) how excited are you? You might be thinking, "Oh my God, I can no wait to implement. This is so awesome. I was already familiar with most of the resources she mentioned and the ones I was not I can look up later. I now know how to use them in a brand-new way."

Or you might be thinking, "Oh my God, I don't know any of those resources or platforms. I'm more than a little overwhelmed because I don't know how to put it all together. I don't know how to use Word. I don't know how to take what I do and make into an audiobook or an e-Book. How do I do that? How do I get it transcribed? How much do I pay for that service because I don't want to overpay? What do I do? I don't know how to do all those things. Catherine, help me!"

Well if you are getting started in this marketplace thing or just would love a step by step, screen share, real time answers to your questions, a group atmosphere and access to my network of experts then my friend The Teach Your Easy Virtual Retreat is for you. I made it super easy, very accessible and completable (if that is a word).

This is my invitation to you. If you need more help. If you want me to show you how to use Canva. If you want to see how long it should take you to complete each task - because maybe you think it should take weeks when in reality it should take hours. Again, I spoke my audiobook in less than 3-hours - but if you are thinking, "Of course it only took you two and half hours to complete Catherine. You know how to do that thing."

Yes, that is true, but I too had to learn at some point. I had to. So, if you need more help, and know that if you don't have a set time on your calendar when other people are also going to show up to the work it probably won't happen.

I can show you how to use the Voice Record App. I can also show you how to record your audio program in a more advanced way by using GarageBand (for mac users). I will tell you which microphone to buy from Amazon and how I put all the pieces together.

I brushed on my Garage Band skills because I had not used it in a while; three years to be honest, I literally spent 20-minutes reviewing how to use it. And then I just launched the app and began recording the audiobook. How do you do that? I want to show you how to do that as well.

As you can see, there are resources and training for both beginners and advanced course and content creators. Check out the information page: http://www.teachyoureasy.com/virtualretreat and take advantage of this amazing virtual retreat and awesome package.

WHAT'S INCLUDED IN THE TEACH YOUR EASY VIRTUAL RETREAT? I AM GLAD YOU ASKED, SEE BELOW:

3-days of hands on learning and implementation Sessions ($997 value)

We will work together; I will give you guidance, concrete steps to take, and then provide the space for you to implement. When questions come up, and they will; I will be there to answer them.

Complete Advanced list of resources and platforms ($197 value)

Don't waste time searching for the right vendors to help you with editing, formatting, graphics or admin work; I will share my private list of platforms and freelancer's rolodex.

30-day Sales & Marketing Accountability Private Group ($247 value)

One you have your product, course or service created you will need the accountability and support to share it with the world. I wish I had that every time I launched a new book or course.

All three-day audio and Video recordings ($997 value)

Whether you are creating another product or want to get a refresher of some or all the sessions you will have access to the recordings.

Rapid-Fire Hot seats ($597 value)

Not sure what your product, service or course should be? Or need to get clarity on your idea? Then these rapid-fire hot seats will come in handy for you.

Bonus: Why your content/biz/ministry or product is bombing & How to Turn it Around (valued at $97)

This short but powerful resource will help you see the areas that need changing and how to adjust them so your ministry and business can grow.

Bonus: Access to The Confidence Unchained Course (valued at $247)

Putting yourself out there it's not easy and I know having the confidence to show up fully is non- negotiable. That's why I KNEW I had to gift you this course. It is SO powerful.

Bonus: Group Q&A Session inside of private community (valued at $497)

After the virtual retreat you will have SO many questions (totally normal and understandable) but worry not, I got you. You will be able to post ALL your questions in our private community and then I will host a group Q&A video session to respond.

CONCLUSION

We have had a blast in this Teach Your Easy journey, haven't we? We have gone through every step with care and hopefully you had fun along the way. The stuff that I just taught you came to me in a little over two hours because it is my easy. I broke it down for you too. And I love the fact that God allows me to demonstrate what that formula looks like by sharing my own story; by telling you what my struggles used to be. Being human and not pretending to be someone I am not; just telling you what happened. How my life has changed by showing you how I have been helping people for the last few years with strategies, resources and with my nerdiness.

Now you can do this. I have no doubt in my mind that you can do this because I just taught you, and not only did I teach you, I spoke this over your life. You didn't even know that I was getting in your head. Now every time you are about to do something, you will ask yourself, "Oh, can I monetize that? What would Catherine do? Would Catherine monetize this? I think she would. I'm going to create a program." Then you'll start typing like a crazy person and create a program, an E-book or how-to book.

I believe you can do this because I can do it. I showed you how. I walked you through the process step by step. How very awesome is that? I'm so excited for you and cannot wait to hear how you turn all the things I taught you into money. Literally, you are on your way to making money on the regular, how awesome is that? I'm so happy that I was able to do this, spending this time with you. I had a blast. I love teaching; it's my favorite and it has been my honor to spend this time with you.

This is my easy, and I pray that I have made it easy for you to learn as well.

Why did I create written, visual, and audio versions of the program? Because I wanted to cover all the senses so I could teach my audience in the way they prefer to learn. You can do the same when you create your program. However, you don't have to start with all those versions from the beginning. You can start with one and add more as you course, program or service begins to sell. Pace yourself and have fun along the way.

Thank you so much for reading this manual. It has been a pleasure and an honor. I'm so excited for you, because if you follow my teaching, do the work and remain consistent you should create some great revenue streams by helping people with YOUR easy.

Thank you so very much. Let's connect on social media, look me up; tell me how this book helped you, blessed your life, changed your life for the better or helped you to make all kinds of money.

I'm a teacher. And I'll be teaching so many more things in the days, weeks and years to come. Why? Because it's easy for me, and I believe that you can teach your easy too. God bless you.

AUTHOR'S BIO

I am a Content Monetization Strategist, Amazon Best-Selling Author of about 20-21 books (who can keep count, right?), Keynote and 2-time TEDx Speaker, founder of Writing Made Simple, Certified Life Coach, Certified Christian Mentor, preacher and woman of faith. I have been coaching others for more than twenty years (even when I did not know it yet). I never thought my love for words, books, and writing would allow me to pool my expertise and help others to bring out their authentic voice and content to the world.

Today I get to work with committed kingdom womenpreneurs, faith-based leaders, executives, and lay professional women (and a few determined men) who are willing and ready to serve others with their words and talents in a global capacity. However, they know they need the confidence, guidance, and tools to successfully embraced their calling and help others by teaching their easy with their content, books, courses, products, and programs.

Connect with Catherine online:

Facebook:
https://www.facebook.com/catherinestoring/

Instagram:
https://www.instagram.com/catherinestoring

YouTube: http://bit.ly/wmsTV

Twitter: https://twitter.com/CatStoring

Website: http://writingmadesimple.today/

NOTES

Lightning Source UK Ltd.
Milton Keynes UK
UKHW011447240219
337804UK00009B/1510/P